WHY

THE DEVIL DOESN'T WANT YOU TO PRAY IN

TONGUES

Roberts Liardon

EMBASSY
PUBLISHING

Irvine, CA

1st Printing

Why The Devil Doesn't Want You To Pray In Tongues
ISBN 1-890900-34-6

Published by Embassy Publishing Co.
P.O. Box 3500
Laguna Hills, CA 92654

CONTENTS

1

WELCOME TO THE WONDERFUL WORLD OF TONGUES

While preaching in New York a few years back, I had one of the most unique experiences of my life. I received a phone call from a couple of pastors in Long Island who wanted me to come and share my Heaven testimony at an evangelistic crusade they were holding.

"Brother Roberts, we feel like you're supposed to be the one to give the message and throw the net of salvation," they said.

"I'd love to do it," I responded.

When I flew in, they picked me up and took me to the hotel where they were holding the meeting. The meeting was on neutral turf in a hotel ball room that seated about 500 people. I had arrived a little late so I quickly changed my clothes and went downstairs to join the meeting that was already in progress. Every seat was taken. There were even people in the back of the room standing — the house was packed.

When I stepped behind the pulpit, I began by telling the people how the Lord showed me a part of Heaven when I was a little boy. I told them what I saw and how I felt, as I normally do when I share my Heaven testimony.

As I was speaking, I noticed a lady sitting about 5 rows back and beside her were three teenagers dressed in black leather and chains. The way these teenagers dressed didn't bug me, but they were the only people in the building dressed like that, so they kind of stood out.

Usually, it takes me about 40 to 45 minutes to tell my heaven story and then about 20 minutes to give the altar call. But about 30 minutes into my message, the Lord interrupted me.

"Call those three young men out and have them stand in front of you," He said.

I had enough sense to obey God, but I was real apprehensive about it.

"You three, come up here please," I said, pointing my finger as confidently as I could in their direction.

To my surprise, they got up, they walked straight down the aisle and stood in front of the pulpit. I didn't know what God wanted me to do next so I just stood there awhile as they looked at me.

I looked at them.

They looked at each other.

They looked at me again.

I looked back at them.

I was getting *real* uncomfortable!

I was trying to act spiritual because that's what you do when you don't know what else to do! I knew enough about obeying the Holy Spirit to only do what He said, but it seemed like He had left me hanging.

So there I was, standing in front of 500 New Yorkers trying to look spiritual when all of a sudden, the woman I had noticed earlier fell out of her chair, face forward, in the middle of the aisle! She fell over with a loud thud and scared the whole crowd!

There were no "cloth workers" in that meeting and when the lady fell over, her dress was hiked up a little bit. It wasn't up too high, but it was enough to make me nervous!

By this time we were so far into this strange event that there was no way out. I couldn't sermonize it and I couldn't praise my way out of the situation. I had to just flow with it.

I knew it was God, but I didn't want to look at the pastors because I was sure my days of Long Island ministry had come to an abrupt conclusion! They had wanted an evangelistic meeting. They didn't want a woman shot out of a chair in the middle of the aisle with her nose buried in the carpet! The woman didn't even move! She just laid there! The three guys in leather looked at her, then looked at me, looked at her again and then looked back at me. I just tried to keep looking spiritual!

On the outside I was smiling but on the inside I was saying, "Help me God! Show up, show up, show up! Please show up and help me out of this mess!"

(It seems funny now, but it wasn't funny then!)

Then there came another surprise! The woman who had her nose buried in the carpet began to pray loudly in the most unusual tongue I'd ever heard in my life. It sounded like a mixture of Chinese and some kind of strange African dialect. She prayed in that unusual sounding tongue for about 10 minutes without stopping.

The Bible says, "Watch and pray," so I watched and she prayed! And the whole crowd watched too! Nobody went to the bathroom, nobody left to go home early, and not one baby in the room cried. No one moved.

Suddenly, one of the three teenagers that was in front of me fell flat on the floor. It startled me and I jumped. All my attention had been on the woman who was laying on her face in the aisle — I had forgotten about the three guys in leather! When the boy fell over, he rolled up in a little ball and began to cry with deep, gut-wrenching sobs.

So now there were *two* shows going on in the room! A woman on her face in the aisle praying in unusual sounding tongues and a teenager dressed in leather, rolled up in a little ball crying!

This went on for 15 minutes or so. I just stood and watched. When the woman wouldn't pray as strong, the young man would stop crying and try to catch his breath. When she would begin praying hard, he would start crying again. They'd go at it in 3 or 4 minute rounds. Whenever the woman would pray in tongues fervently, the teenager would cry like somebody was beating him up! I was raised as a Pentecostal and I had seen some unusual things, but I had never seen anything like this before!

About 45 minutes into this dramatic episode, the woman suddenly stopped praying and sat up on her knees and raised her hands half-way up to the Lord. As she knelt there with her eyes closed, her makeup all goofed up and one clip-on earring hanging out of place, she began singing in tongues and interpreting her tongues back to herself.

Then, without warning, she got up like everything was normal, sat down on her chair, closed her eyes and calmly laid her hands in her lap.

When I looked over at the three teenagers dressed in leather, the crying boy's two friends had moved back to the sides to get away from what was happening.

Finally, after catching his breath, the young man on the floor lifted up his head and tried to focus his eyes. When he had regained enough strength to get up, he walked over to the edge of the platform where I was standing. Tilting his head, he looked up at me all sweaty and red-faced and said, "Sir, I think I need to get saved."

Suddenly the crowd went wild in rejoicing! They acted like someone had just scored a touchdown at a football game!

This young man was saved and filled with the Holy Spirit that night. It was almost as though God had orchestrated that entire meeting just for him!

God Knows What Kind Of Prayer Is Needed

Why did I take time to tell you this story? Because you need to know that God gives you diversities of tongues to bring victory in every situation you're facing! In this woman's case, the Holy Spirit knew what kind of intercession, what level of intensity and what type of divine expression was needed to get this young man delivered.

I found out after the meeting that the teenager was the woman's son. His father had hurt him deeply when he divorced his mother. This teenager began to get rebellious and would not come home sometimes on the weekends. The mother had tried everything to help her son including counseling, but he only got worse. Thank God she knew about the diversities of tongues! The Holy Spirit helped her to pray in a way that brought a great victory to her family.

Welcome To The World Of Tongues

The world of tongues and their diversities is one of the spiritual frontiers that God's children are still pressing into. There is more to the world of praying in tongues than anyone has yet discovered. If the Lord tarries and we all live to see death, we still will have not exhausted the subject of speaking in unknown tongues.

The purpose of this book is to help you gain accurate revelation concerning the role of tongues and their diversities in your life and ministry. I wrote it to help you understand that the baptism in the Holy Spirit with the evidence of speaking in tongues should be a *normal* part of your Christian life and that speaking in tongues with all their diversities helps you to be more normal than you've ever been before!

The devil doesn't want you to pray in tongues, my brother and sister! He wants to keep you ignorant of tongues and their diversities so the Holy Spirit's power won't be able to flow through you as it should.

Everybody in the world needs to receive the baptism in the Holy Ghost with the evidence of speaking in other tongues. As we will see, there is nothing more beautiful than having a heavenly language flow out of an earthen vessel to do a supernatural work.

We will begin our scriptural journey into the wonderful world of tongues by exploring what Jesus said about the Holy Spirit.

2

WHAT JESUS SAID ABOUT THE HOLY SPIRIT

"If ye love me, keep my commandments. And I will pray the Father, and HE SHALL GIVE YOU ANOTHER COMFORTER, that he may abide with you for ever; Even the Spirit of truth; whom the world cannot receive, because it seeth him not, neither knoweth him: but ye know him; for he dwelleth with you, and shall be in you."

John 14:15-17 (KJV)

"The Comforter" was one of the terms Jesus used to describe the Holy Spirit. In this scripture, the disciples were being prepared for a great transition; Jesus was about to leave the earth and the Holy Spirit was about to be poured out. Notice here that Jesus said that the Father would give the disciples, *"another comforter...."* (John 14:16) Who was the first Comforter? Jesus was! The disciples looked to Jesus as their helper, guide and teacher. Jesus confronted them, loved them, instructed them, strengthened them and revealed things to them. What Jesus was to the disciples, the Holy Spirit is to you and me today.

Not A Fair-Weathered Friend

Jesus went on to say that the Comforter would, *"abide with you forever."* (John 14:16) That means He's not going to fly away. The Holy Spirit is like super glue; He sticks to you! He'll *never* leave you or forsake you! (John 14:18; Heb 13:5)

Now if you consistently resist the Holy Spirit and run to do evil, He'll eventually let you do it, but He will always be there to help you if you'll cry out to Him.

It's good to know that the Holy Spirit abides with you forever. That means that He will be with you through the thick and the thin — the good times *and* the bad times. The Holy Spirit is not a fair-weathered friend! It doesn't matter whether the sun is out and everything is fine, or whether you're facing the greatest challenge of your life; He'll never act like a distant relative!

The Spirit And The World Don't Date

"...he shall give you another Comforter, that he may abide with you for ever; EVEN THE SPIRIT OF TRUTH;

WHOM THE WORLD CANNOT RECEIVE..." (John 14:16-17)

Religious devils and worldly folks lie at times and try to deceive you, but the Holy Spirit *cannot* lie. He is the Spirit of Truth.

Notice Jesus said that the Holy Spirit was the Spirit *"whom the world cannot receive."* (Verse 17) The Holy Spirit and the spirit of the world don't date, my brother and sister! They don't have midnight rendezvous! In fact, they don't get along at all! If you're filled with the Holy Spirit, you won't have a love for the things of this present world. (1 Jn 2:15) There won't be a mixture of the world and the Holy Spirit in you.

"Well, I love the Lord, but I do what I want during the week."

And you're a fool too! If you live like that, you're a religious backslider! Some people will go to hell with their prayer beads in their hand, saying, "But I was praying!" Yes, but you never lived the Christian life and got right with God! You just played religious games!

"Well, I go to church!"

So what? The devil goes to church and even sings in the choir! Don't use that as an excuse to ease your conscience!

"Yes, but my grandmother is a prayer person."

Well, *she'll* probably go to Heaven, but *you* won't unless you get right with God for yourself.

"Well she'll pray me into Heaven."

That's not the way it works. No one can pray you into Heaven, my friend! They can pray you into the consciousness of what it will take to get to Heaven, but they can't "piggyback" you into heaven. You have to get it for yourself! You have to fall at the foot of the cross, cry out to God and get cleansed with the blood of Jesus Christ! You have to get right with Him and you have to do it for yourself.

"Well they're praying for me."

It's good that they're praying for you; they're probably holding back a lot of self-inflicted troubles.

Johnny Carson Meets Kathryn Kuhlman

The Holy Spirit is called the Spirit of Truth, *"whom the world cannot receive."* You see, the world cannot receive the Spirit of Truth unless they call upon the Lord and receive Him as Savior. They cannot receive the Holy Spirit because those in the world *"seeth Him not."* Sinners live by sense knowledge, but Christians live by faith in the Bible and in their inward witness.

Johnny Carson, the famous late-night talk show host, once asked Kathryn Kuhlman how she knew when the Holy Spirit was in the room.

"You can feel Him," she said.

"Yes, but you can't see Him."

"You can't see the wind either," she responded, "but you know when the wind is blowing. You can feel the wind and you can watch it blow things around. It's the same with the Holy Spirit. When the Holy Spirit is in the room, you'll start seeing manifestations of His presence. People will cry and humble themselves before the Lord. They'll get healed, devils will come out and the gifts of the Spirit will begin manifesting."

He Will Guide You Into All Truth

In John chapter 16, we read something else that Jesus said about the Holy Spirit.

"I still have many things to say to you, but you cannot bear them now. However, when He, the Spirit of truth, has come, He will guide you into all truth; for He will not speak on His own authority, but whatever He hears He will speak; and He will tell you things to come."

John 16:12-13 (NKJ)

Notice Jesus said, *"I still have many things to say to you, but you cannot bear them now."* There's a lot the Holy Spirit would reveal to people, but He can't because they aren't preparing themselves for it. You have to position yourself correctly in the natural and in the spirit if you want to partake of the deeper things of God. (1 Cor 2:10)

He Will Guide You Into All Victory

"Howbeit when He, the Holy Spirit, the Spirit of truth is come, He will guide you into all truth." (John 16:13) "All truth" is another way of saying, "all victory." The Holy Spirit will never guide you into defeat! He will always guide you into victory, success, accomplishment, abundant life, soundness, happiness and security; both in the spirit and in the natural. He'll tell you what decisions to make in business so you won't go broke every other month. He'll tell you who *not* to do business with so you can have peace of mind when you go home to kiss your wife and hug the kids. He'll tell you whether your $20,000 investment is going to profit you or whether you're going to lose it all. He'll tell you what house to buy, when to buy it and how much to pay! When the Holy Spirit is helping you, you'll get a good deal no matter what the real estate agents have to say about it!

The Holy Spirit will show you what to do in every circumstance of life. He will even show you where to have a nice vacation! Sometimes He will say, "No, don't go there this year, go here instead." That happened to me. I was going to visit some friends and take a little vacation and the Holy Spirit said, "No, don't go there at this time, it's not right. Go some place else." He didn't tell me where to go,

He just told me go somewhere else. I had a great vacation that year, too. I really enjoyed it. If I had disobeyed the Holy Spirit, I probably would have ended up in the middle of some difficulty. I didn't ask the Holy Spirit *why* He wanted me to go somewhere else because I really didn't want to know. I just obeyed Him and had a good time.

The Holy Spirit doesn't always reveal the intimate details of a situation, because in some cases, *it's none of your business.* He only tells you what He wants you to know and nothing else. You just have to relax and trust Him. If He says, "No don't do that right now," then just obey Him and be happy about it. Trust Him. He will never lead you into failure, defeat, error or deception. He's there to protect your life, not destroy it.

Notice that Jesus said, *"He will guide you...."* (John 16:13) That means the Holy Spirit will not pick you up and sovereignly place you in the will of God. He will only help you to get there. He will show you which roads to take and which roads to avoid. If you'll listen to Him, He will get you to where you belong. He'll never lead you astray.

He Will Show You Things To Come

Jesus goes on to say that the Holy Spirit, *"...will not speak of Himself."* (John 16:13) That means that the Holy Spirit doesn't have an ego problem. He doesn't fly around saying, "I was there when the world was made! I'm just as big as the Father! I deserve some of the credit for all of this because I'm the Holy Spirit!" The Holy Spirit doesn't act like humans. He doesn't have a pride problem at all. He has come for two main purposes: *to reveal Jesus in the earth and to empower believers.* He has come to be your guide, your comforter and your helper in life and it's up to you to let Him do it.

"He will not speak of Himself, but whatsoever He shall hear, that shall He speak, and He will show you things to come." (John 16:13)

Who is the Holy Spirit listening to? He's listening to the Father and He's listening to the Son. Whatever He hears them saying, He will reveal to you. If you're real close to Him, He will sometimes let you in on things that are being planned by the Father and the Son. He'll give you glimpses into what is being sent from Heaven to the earth. The Holy Spirit has access to that kind of communication between the Father and the Son. He has the ability to observe and know what's being planned, because He's a part of it. Jesus said that the Holy Spirit would show you things to come. That means that the Holy Spirit will show you things to come on different levels of life. He will show you things to come in your family. He will show you things to come in the church. He will show you things to come in your community, in the nation, in the world and in the realm of the spirit. The Holy Spirit will roll back the curtains of the future and show you what's about to take place. He likes doing that, because that's what Jesus sent Him to do.

Tribulation Trouble

Every Christian should have an inner awareness of the future and not just a generic paranoia of end time prophecy.

"Well 666 is here and the government is getting ready to stamp it on our foreheads!"

Maybe so, but the Holy Spirit is planning to have a revival first! Some of these end-time prophecy teachers jump over the work of the kingdom and try to get everyone living in the tribulation before the time!

"Well, we are closer to the tribulation, aren't we?"

Yes, but why focus on that? We should be focused on getting people saved, building new churches and going to the mission field while we still have time.

"But we should be aware that the Lord is coming!"

Of course! But that should also make us realize that it's time to get to work. I'd rather be found laboring in the harvest field than looking at the sky through a pair of binoculars!

In verse 14, Jesus said, *"...and He will glorify Me...."* In other words, the Holy Spirit will lift up Jesus. He will reveal Jesus to you and show you how to make Jesus your personal friend. *"For He shall receive of Mine and shall show it unto you."* (John 16:14)

3

WHAT HAPPENED WHEN THE HOLY SPIRIT CAME

And when the day of Pentecost was fully come, they were all with one accord in one place. And suddenly there came a sound from heaven as of a rushing mighty wind, and it filled all the house where they were sitting. And there appeared unto them cloven tongues like as of fire, and it sat upon each of them. And they were all filled with the Holy Spirit, and began to speak with other tongues, as the Spirit gave them utterance.

Acts 2:1-4 (KJV)

Notice here in verse 1 that the disciples were *"with one accord and one place."* Now that's a miracle by itself! To get that many Christians in one accord usually takes a sovereign act of God!

God is wanting His people to come into the true unity of the Spirit. True unity is not just outward conformity, it is established in our hearts through the inner workings of God. Many in the Catholic church dress in black and white outfits, but that doesn't mean they're unified, it just means they all dress the same. True unity is an inward unity of vision and purpose which the entire body of Christ should be united under.

No Tarrying Needed

Jesus had commanded the disciples to "tarry" in Jerusalem for the promise of the Holy Spirit. (Luke 24:49)

Many Christians today get hung up on the "tarrying" doctrine. Some tarry so long that they die without receiving the promise of the Spirit! The disciples tarried in the book of Acts because they were waiting for the promise of the Holy Spirit. Now that we are on the other side of Pentecost, there is no need to tarry to receive the Holy Spirit, because He's come!

The Holy Spirit's Arrival

"And suddenly there came a sound from heaven as of a rushing mighty wind...." (Acts 2:2)

The word *"rushing"* indicates that the Holy Spirit was in a hurry to get here. He didn't fly around Jupiter, visit Mars, and then circle the sun for a little vacation! He came straight from Heaven at an accelerated pace. He couldn't wait to get here; to baptize us, to fill us, to teach us, to guide us and to help us. This shows us the Holy Spirit's earnest desire to provide us with His divine assistance.

The word *"mighty"* shows us that He didn't come like Casper the friendly ghost — He came with great strength and power! He came as a *"rushing mighty wind and it filled the whole house where they were sitting."* (Acts 2:2) This shows us that *strength* is one of the predominate characteristics of the Holy Spirit's personality. When Jesus was baptized in the Holy Spirit in Matthew chapter three, the Holy Spirit came upon Him gently in the form of a dove. (Mat 3:16) But on the day of Pentecost, the Holy Spirit came in the form of a *"rushing mighty wind..."* (Acts 2:2) This shows the dual personality of the Holy Spirit. There is a gentle side to Him and there is a mighty side. We have to be willing for *both* to manifest through us at different times.

They All Spoke In Tongues

In verse 3 we read: *"Then there appeared to them DIVIDED TONGUES, AS OF FIRE, and one sat upon each of them."* (Acts 2:3) The holy fire of God's anointing sparks a supernatural zeal and it also has a purifying effect. It will burn up the "chaff" in your life and give you strength to live holy before God.

"And they were ALL filled with the Holy Spirit and begun to speak with other tongues, AS THE SPIRIT GAVE THEM UTTERANCE." (Acts 2:4)

What did the 120 do when they were filled with the Holy Spirit? They began to speak in tongues! How many of them spoke? ALL of them!

"Now Brother Roberts, you don't want to go too far."

Yes I do! I want to go all the way with God! I want to get everyone I meet filled with the Spirit with the evidence of speaking in other tongues! The scriptures are clear; when you are baptized, or filled to overflowing with the Holy Spirit, you will speak in other tongues. If you don't speak in other tongues, then you're not *full* of the Holy Spirit. It's that simple. You may be *indwelled* by the Spirit and have an inner witness that you are a child of God — He may work with you a little bit according to the level you allow Him — but you're not *filled* with the Holy Spirit.

The Bible says, *"They were all filled with the Holy Spirit, AND..."* The word *and* is a conjunction; it means that whatever follows goes with whatever preceded it. *"AND they began to speak with other tongues."* (Acts 2:4)

"Brother Roberts, are you saying that I'm a second rate Christian if I have not been baptized in the Holy Spirit and speak with other tongues?"

No! But I *am* saying that the Holy Spirit is not in you to full capacity.

"Well you're making me a second rate Christian."

No, I'm trying to get you to receive all that God has freely provided. The baptism in the Holy Spirit with the evidence of speaking in tongues is rightfully yours as a child of God.

I believe that some Christians who are filled with the Holy Spirit have not yet released the speaking in tongues part. This is mainly because of an absence of knowledge. But I believe that the full baptism of the Holy Spirit is always evidenced by speaking in tongues. You'll see that this is true as we examine different portions of Scripture in the next chapter.

4

THE HOLY SPIRIT & TONGUES IN THE BOOK OF ACTS

Let's look at some examples of the baptism in the Holy Spirit with the evidence of tongues in the book of Acts. In Acts chapter 10 verses 44-46 we read:

While Peter was still speaking these words, the Holy Spirit fell upon all those who heard the word. And those of the circumcision who believed were astonished, as many as came with Peter, because the gift of the Holy Spirit had been poured out on the Gentiles also. For they heard them speak with tongues and magnify God.

Acts 10:44-46 (NKJ)

The hearing of the Word causes the Holy Spirit to move. You'll notice throughout the New Testament that whenever people heard the Word, they were saved, healed and delivered. Here in this scripture, when the gentiles heard the Word preached to them, they received the *"gift"* of the Holy Spirit. The term *"gift"* implies that the Holy Spirit is free — you can't buy Him — all you can do is receive Him.

So what happened when these gentiles received the Holy Spirit? We find the answer in Acts 10 verse 46: *"For they heard them speak with tongues and magnify God."* Speaking in tongues helps your magnification of God. Notice that receiving the Holy Spirit and speaking in tongues are received together in the same experience.

"For they heard them," that's the opposite of not hearing. Notice that they were speaking loud enough for those who were with Peter to be astonished that the gentiles now were speaking in tongues.

There are people who think this way today. They say, "Well only special people can speak in tongues. It's not for us." This scripture tells us that, after receiving salvation, *anybody* can receive the Holy Spirit and speak with other tongues!

If you're truly filled with the Holy Spirit, you will pray in other tongues loud enough for everyone to say, "What's that?"

Now if you're born again, you'll have the witness of the Spirit within you and the Spirit will help you according to level you allow Him. But if you want to be empowered to the full capacity that the Lord desires, you need to receive the Holy Spirit and pray in other tongues; boldly and unashamedly. Please underline that in your

Bible, *"For they HEARD them speak with tongues and magnify God."* (Acts 10:46)

Witness Number Two

The Bible says that, *"In the mouth of two or three witnesses let everything be established."* (2 Cor 13:1) So let's look at another scripture.

And it happened, while Apollos was at Corinth, that Paul, having passed through the upper regions, came to Ephesus. And finding some disciples he said to them, "Did you receive the Holy Spirit when you believed?" So they said to him, "We have not so much as heard whether there is a Holy Spirit." And he said to them, "Into what then were you baptized?" So they said, "Into John's baptism." Then Paul said, "John indeed baptized with a baptism of repentance, saying to the people that they should believe on Him who would come after him, that is, on Christ Jesus." When they heard this, they were baptized in the name of the Lord Jesus. And when Paul had laid hands on them, the Holy Spirit came upon them, and they spoke with tongues and prophesied.

Acts 19:1-6 (NKJ)

Sometimes, when I read about the way Paul lived in the book of Acts, I think, "Lord, that sounds so exciting." Paul *found* this group of disciples, which means he didn't know they were there.

Because these men believed in John's preaching, they easily received what Paul had to say about the Holy Spirit. Notice that it was important to Paul to make sure that these disciples were filled with the Holy Spirit. It wasn't an afterthought, the first thing he said to them was, *"Have you received the Holy Spirit since you have believed?"* (Acts 19:2)

"We don't know whether there be any Holy Spirit."

Their answer probably caught Paul off guard.

"What baptism are you baptized under?" Paul responded. "John's baptism."

These disciples had not been around the occurrence of the upper room. So Paul said, *"John truly baptized with the baptism of repentance, but do you remember what John said? He said that you are to believe on the One that comes after him, and that One is Jesus Christ."* (Acts 19:4)

What did the disciples do after Paul told them about the Holy Spirit? They believed! And what happened when they received the Holy Spirit? They spoke with tongues and prophesied!

So this is your third "witness": *"The Holy Spirit came upon them, they spoke with tongues and prophesied."* (Acts 19:6) But that's not all; I have another witness for you. In the next chapter we will see that even the great Apostle Paul spoke in tongues when he received the Holy Spirit.

5

PAUL & HIS EXPERIENCE WITH THE HOLY SPIRIT & TONGUES

In Acts chapter 9, we find the story of Paul's conversion. In verse 4, we read that Paul has been knocked off his horse, he's gone blind and he's had a vision all at the same time — *now that's called an event!* It gets even more dramatic when you consider Paul's occupation before this occurrence; he was persecuting the Christians, putting them in jail, and killing them! Then God sent His lightnings from His throne room and interrupted Paul's evil agenda. Everybody that was with Paul fell to the earth but Paul was the only one who heard and saw Jesus.

Let's begin reading from verse 8:

Then Saul arose from the ground, and when his eyes were opened he saw no one. But they led him by

the hand and brought him into Damascus. And he was
three days without sight, and neither ate nor drank.

Acts 9:8-9 (NKJ)

After an experience like that, I don't think I'd eat or drink either! Think of this poor man's shock factor! He's on his horse, traveling to the next city and looking for Christians to persecute and ... bam! He wakes up after a vision and he can't see a thing! For three days and three nights, he does nothing but fast and pray. I think that's kind of funny! I'd pray too if I was knocked off my horse and struck blind! I'd pray loud enough for the whole world to hear! That's what Paul did at the beginning of his experience with Jesus.

Let's continue reading in verse 10:

Now there was a certain disciple at Damascus
named Ananias; and to him the Lord said in a vision,
"Ananias." And he said, "Here I am, Lord."

Acts 9:10 (NKJ)

I'm so glad that there are men of maturity in the Spirit who can respond properly during a heavenly visitation. In the scriptures, every time angels show up they say, "Fear not!" because most people are overwhelmed by fear and lose it. If an angel appears to you don't say, "Oh my God, there's an angel in front of me, what am I supposed to do?" Just cool your jets and say, "What's up?" Or just stand there and listen to what he has to say.

You can tell Ananias was mature by the way he responded during the visitation. He said, "Here I am Lord!" In other words he was saying, "I'm available! What is it that you want me to do?"

So the Lord said to him, "Arise and go to the street called Straight, and inquire at the house of Judas for one called Saul of Tarsus, for behold, he is praying. And in a vision he has seen a man named Ananias coming in and putting his hand on him, so that he might receive his sight."

Acts 9:11-12 (NKJ)

Here in this account of Paul's conversion experience, we see that he has two visions within the first few hours of his salvation experience. The one that knocked him off his high horse and the one that brought comfort to him showing that God was going to take care of his blindness.

Then Ananias answered, "Lord, I have heard much about this man. He has done great harm to Your saints in Jerusalem. I hear he has authority from the chief priests to bind all who call on Your name."

But the Lord said to him, "Go, for he is a chosen vessel of Mine to bear My name before Gentiles, kings, and the children of Israel. For I will show him how many things he must suffer for My name's sake."

And Ananias went his way and entered the house; and laying his hands on him he said, "Brother Saul, the Lord Jesus, who appeared to you on the road as you came, has sent me that you may receive your sight and be filled with the Holy Spirit."

Acts 9:13-17 (NKJ)

Notice here in verse 17 that Paul was filled the Holy Spirit when this great servant laid his hands upon him. Some use this particular verse as an excuse not to speak in tongues when they receive the baptism in the Holy Spirit because it does not actually say here that Paul spoke in tongues. But Paul wrote more about tongues than anybody else in the Bible. In First Corinthians 14 and verse 18 Paul writes: *"I thank my God I speak in tongues more than you all."* It is obvious by that statement that Paul prayed in tongues a whole lot.

Paul wrote this Epistle to bring the Corinthian believers into order because of wrong activities and the misuse of certain things. He offered them his instructions in these chapters to help them use tongues more effectively.

Some people have tried to use Paul's writings to discourage people from speaking in tongues. But Paul was not beating the Corinthians down, he was just giving them instructions so that tongues could be more beneficial in their life.

I Want To Start A Holy Competition

I have a holy competition going between me and the apostle Paul and I won't know if I win it until I get to Heaven. I want it to be said of me that Roberts Liardon prayed in tongues more than all of them including the apostle Paul! I think that's a holy and good competition and I want to enlist you! Let's all try to outdo Paul.

"How will we know when we've done it?"

We won't know until we get to Heaven, so just keep doing it and then when we all get there we'll see who won!

Tongues Was Normal To Paul

I believe that when Ananias laid his hands on Paul, Paul was filled with the Holy Spirit and began to speak in other tongues. Why would Paul's infilling of the Holy Spirit be different than all the others in the book of Acts?

So that verse and this verse constitutes that the apostle Paul spoke with tongues. And if the apostle Paul spoke with tongues, then we should speak with tongues, too!

Paul didn't speak in tongues just one time, either. When Paul says, *"I'm glad I speak in tongues more than you all,"* (1 Cor 14:18) he gives us the understanding that this was a continual occurrence in his life. Tongues was something that was normal to Paul — it was something he flowed with daily.

6

THE BENEFITS OF PRAYING IN TONGUES

If you've been to any of my meetings, you know that I'm a strong advocate of the development of people's prayer lives; especially in the area of praying in tongues. I emphasize tongues and strong prayer during my messages often because I know how beneficial these things are to a Christian's life. Here are just a few of the benefits of praying in tongues.

1) Tongues is a Sign

The first benefit of speaking in tongues is that it gives you the assurance that you've been baptized in the Holy Spirit. In my meetings, I often urge those in the congregation to ask the folks next to them if they are saved and filled with the Spirit. Sometimes I will even tell them to ask the person beside them to pray in tongues out loud.

If that person is filled with the Holy Spirit, tongues will flow right out of them. If they're not filled with the Spirit, I will call them forward to receive the baptism. I call that going fishing!

2) Tongues Will Make You Strong

Another scriptural reason for praying in tongues is that it makes your spirit strong in 1st Corinthians 14 verse 4 we read:

He who speaks in a tongue edifies himself…

1 Cor 14:4 (NKJ)

The word "edify" here means to make you spiritually strong. Praying in tongues helps you to become spiritually fit so you can carry out the works of God in the earth. If you have a whimpy spirit, it's possible that you're not praying in tongues enough.

Do you remember that commercial in America a few years ago about Hefty trash bags? It was either "Whimpy, Whimpy, Whimpy," or "Hefty, Hefty, Hefty." You have to decide what kind of container you want to be, a whimpy one, or a hefty three-ply one. I want to be a hefty three-ply container so I can hold a lot of God's mighty power!

3) Tongues Makes You Spiritually Sensitive

Praying in tongues helps you become aware of spiritual events and occurrences. It helps you increase your sensitivity to the workings of the Holy Spirit. People that don't pray in tongues much are not as sharp as they could be in their discerning of the moves of the Holy Spirit and the overall happenings of God.

4) Tongues Will Build Your Faith

In Jude, verse 20 we find that tongues stirs up our faith. Jude writes:

But you, beloved, building yourselves up on your most holy faith, praying in the Holy Spirit...

Jude 1:20 (NKJ)

Tongues makes your faith come alive! When you get through praying in tongues, you're ready to believe God for anything! It stimulates your ability to trust Him.

5) Tongues Helps To Clean Up Your Mouth

Praying in the Spirit helps you control the wildest member of your body — your tongue!

Your tongue does more than just taste ice cream, my brother and sister! It brings life or death, blessing or cursing, depending on how you let it be used. (Prov 18:21) One of the signs of Christian maturity is how much control you have over the conduct of your mouth.

When you pray in tongues a lot, it makes it easier to keep your mouth in subjection to the Holy Spirit. In other words, it helps to break the unruliness of your tongue and clean up your foul talk.

I know that most Christians don't cuss, but bad confessions and unbelief come out of everyone's mouth from time to time. In light of scripture, unbelief is just as bad as cussing. When you pray in tongues regularly, gossip and accusation will begin to disappear from your speech and holiness will begin to permeate your words and actions.

In James the 1st chapter, verse 26, it says, *"If any man among you seem to be religious,"* (or spiritual), *"and bridleth not his tongue, but deceiveth his own heart, this man's religion is in vain."*

In James the 3rd chapter, verse 8, we read, *"But the tongue can no man tame; it is unruly evil, full of deadly poison."*

If you are always telling people things you shouldn't be telling them, that means you're not yielding your mouth enough to the Lord. Praying in tongues helps you develop an awareness of the conduct of your mouth.

If there was no other benefit to praying in tongues than just to keep your tongue under control, then that would be reason enough to do it.

6) Tongues Brings A Spiritual Refreshing

In Isaiah 28 we see that speaking in tongues brings a spiritual refreshing. In verse 11 we read:

For with stammering lips and another tongue will he speak to this people. To whom he said, This is the rest wherewith ye may cause the weary to rest; and this is the refreshing: yet they would not hear. But the word of the LORD was unto them precept upon precept, precept upon precept; line upon line, line upon line; here a little, and there a little...

Isa 28:11-13 (KJV)

Someone once approached Smith Wigglesworth and said, "Brother Wigglesworth, don't you ever take a vacation?"

"Everyday," he responded.

"What do you mean?"

"I pray in tongues daily and I get refreshed. That's my vacation, that's my holiday."

Praying in tongues refreshes you. Have you ever felt like you were tired, but there was no reason to be tired? When you feel like that, you need to pray in tongues and cause that refreshing to spring up from inside of your spirit. Weariness and tiredness will go and strength will come to you instead.

One way Christians are supposed to find their rest is by praying in tongues. Praying in tongues helps to keep you fresh, strong, up and happy. If you pray in tongues everyday, you can keep yourself invigorated and refreshed.

7) *Tongues Gives You Power To Be a Witness*

Another benefit of tongues is that it gives you power to be a witness.

"But you shall receive power when the Holy Spirit has come upon you; and you shall be witnesses to Me

in Jerusalem, and in all Judea and Samaria, and to the end of the earth."

Acts 1:8 (NKJ)

Tongues & The Great Commission

Consider the transformation of the disciples after the Holy Spirit's outpouring on the day of Pentecost. (Acts 2) These men, who formerly had denied Jesus, feared the masses, and fought among themselves about who would be the greatest, were suddenly preaching with such boldness that the Bible says they turned the world upside down! (Acts 17:6)

After Peter preached on the day of Pentecost, the Bible says three thousand souls were added to the church that very day! (Acts 2:41) That's powerful witnessing!

Jesus said tongues would play a major role in the Great Commission. In Mark 16 we read:

And He said to them, "Go into all the world and preach the gospel to every creature. He who believes and is baptized will be saved; but he who does not believe will be condemned. And these signs will follow those who believe: In My name they will cast out demons; THEY WILL SPEAK WITH NEW TONGUES…

Mark 16:15-17 (NKJ)

A lot of people think that the Great Commission ends with *"Go into all the world and preach…,"* but it continues.

Notice there in verse 17 that it says, *"And they shall speak with new tongues."*

More conservative Christians would say that speaking in new tongues means having the knowledge of a foreign language. I can see why they would say that. On the day of Pentecost and during the Azusa Street outpouring of 1906, and even at times today, God gave some the ability to supernaturally speak the natural languages of the earth with fluency. This is one side of the baptism of the Holy Spirit that I think our generation needs be open to. God will sometimes grant this type of occurrence with the baptism in the Holy Spirit.

Speaking In The Languages Of The Earth

I remember hearing these kinds of stories from my grandmother and from others who were a part of early Pentecostalism. When some received the baptism in the Holy Spirit, they began to miraculously speak in a foreign language.

In Topeka, Kansas, in the year of 1901, a minister by the name of Charles Parham began to receive the understanding of what it means to be baptized in the Holy Spirit. A woman by the name of Agnes Ozman was the first to receive the baptism of the Holy Spirit under Parham's ministry.[1] When she received her prayer language, she received the ability to speak a perfect Chinese dialect

[1] THE ORIGINS OF THE PENTECOSTAL MOVEMENT, Vinson Synan, Ph.D. ORU Webpage

and write it. This was documented at the time by the United States government. They sent language specialists to Topeka to investigate the outbreak of this phenomena. When the government workers got there, they recorded 20 different languages being spoken, as well as a language they could not interpret.

This happened in the early hours of the Pentecostal movement and I believe that this type of manifestation will begin to happen again in the new millennium.

People also experienced this during the Azusa Street outpouring. Missionaries from Azusa Street were sent to almost every major people group in the world. They believed that whatever earthly language they spoke when they were filled with the Holy Spirit was where they were called to go and preach. If they spoke in an African sounding dialect, they got up, bought a boat ticket and floated over to Africa. When they got off the boat, they spoke their language until somebody understood them and then just went right on preaching.

Some went to China. When they got off the boat and started praying in tongues, their language would activate and the people would start responding! Now that's a call, my brother and sister! That's the way it worked for many of them.

Others were able to speak in a foreign language only periodically and when they got to their mission field, they had to learn the language themselves. Why it worked for some and not others I don't know, but I do believe that when Jesus said, *"And they shall speak with new tongues,"* (Mk 16:17) it included the natural languages of the earth as well as the spiritual languages of the heavens. They work together. This is why the Azusa Street outpouring spread so rapidly throughout the earth. They understood the importance of their prayer language in the role of world evangelism. Speaking in tongues gave them power to be effective witnesses for Christ!

7

YOUR PRAYER LANGUAGE SHOULD GROW

And they were all filled with the Holy Spirit and began to speak with other tongues, as the Spirit gave them utterance.

Acts 2:4 (NKJ)

Notice here that it says that the disciples, *"...BEGAN to speak with other tongues..."* The term, *"began to speak"* indicates that this was *not* a one time occurrence — the practice of speaking in tongues continued in their lives and ministries and did not cease after the day of Pentecost.

Some people, when they first begin to speak in tongues, do not have fluency or a large spiritual vocabulary. They are like little children when they're first learning how to speak; they talk in broken words as they're learning.

Newly Spirit-filled believers may have only one word or utterance and just say it over and over. That's OK. It's part of growth and maturing. But your prayer language should grow. There should be more things coming up from your spirit as the Spirit of God gives you greater fluency.

God gave the prophet Isaiah a glimpse of tongues in their infancy. He writes:

For with stammering lips and another tongue he will speak to this people, To whom He said, "This is the rest with which you may cause the weary to rest," and, "This is the refreshing"; yet they would not hear.

Isa 28:11-12 (NKJ)

Notice that Isaiah uses the words, stammering lips. That's referring to folks who are not quite fluent in the spirit yet. Have you ever seen Christians who pray like that? There is no fluency to their prayer language — they just mutter. Some Christians have been filled with the Holy Spirit for twenty years and they're still saying, "See Jane run. Spot jumped over the ball." To me, that's real sad. Tongues is supposed to be a growing language. Stammering lips are supposed to give way to stronger and deeper utterances.

How To Develop Fluency

Some of you reading this book are not as fluent in tongues as you should be. If you've ever heard someone speak in broken English, you can get an idea of what some

Christians sound like when they pray in the spirit. There's no fluency. It's a beginning, but it's really not a language yet. It's just stammering lips. It's like a baby learning to say, "mom," and "dad." The way the child learns is the same way you're going to learn in the spirit. Your tongues will grow as you keep using them. Just take the heavenly language you have and keep speaking it until it becomes distinct and clear. As your language matures, (which does not take years), God will give you more sounds and utterances.

The same way it works in the natural for school kids learning a new language is the same way it works in the realm of the spirit. The only difference is: *it doesn't take as long.* Everything happens by development — by the exercising of your gift. Paul told Timothy to, *"Stir up the gift of God..."* (2 Tim 1:6) That means exercise it, or use it.

If you have been baptized in the Holy Spirit for ten years and all you have is a few basic utterances or syllables, it's time to grow. I want to encourage you to begin to press in to the Holy Spirit and allow Him to expand your prayer language. Begin to speak in the tongues you have and when the Holy Spirit begins to boil something up that's not quite what you're used to, go ahead and speak it out. Don't let your mind talk you out of it.

Don't always think that rapid tongues is anointed either. You'll pray rapid at times, but other times you'll pray real slow. That usually happens to me right before I kick into groanings and travailings or when I'm picking something up. That may not happen to you, but that's what happens to me. It's different for everybody.

You can become the most fluent "tongue talker" in the Body of Christ if you want to. It's available to "whosoever wills." All you need to do is exercise it.

Pray In Your Native Language

When you're developing your prayer language, don't forget to also pray in your native language to edify your mind. Praying in your native language keeps your mind strong and sound.

When I pray in tongues, many times there will come words in English, too. I just obey and speak them out and then I go right back into praying in tongues. Then words in English will come to me again. I'll say things like, "Extend your hands toward us, oh God! In your hands there is justice and righteousness! Extend them over us, oh God."

Many times, what I am speaking in English is the interpretation of what I am praying in the Spirit. It could also be something different. There's really no hard-fast rules when it comes to the wonderful world of tongues. I try never to declare that these things are an unchanging law, because as soon as I do, the Holy Spirit will do something different!

If you aren't quite fluent in tongues yet, just lift your hands right now and begin to pray in the tongues you have.

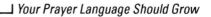

Reach out to God and He will help you increase the free flow of your personal prayer language.

8

TONGUES HELPS OUR INFIRMITIES

Likewise the Spirit also helpeth our infirmities: for we know not what we should pray for as we ought: but the Spirit itself maketh intercession for us with groanings which cannot be uttered. And he that searcheth the hearts knoweth what is the mind of the Spirit, because he maketh intercession for the saints according to the will of God.

Rom 8:26-27 (KJV)

Notice that this scripture says, *"Likewise the Spirit helpeth our infirmities."* If there was ever a verse you needed a revelation of, this is one of them! Out of all the great verses of the Bible, this is one that I hope every Christian gets a revelation of in life. If you can get this verse to come alive inside of you, there is *nothing* you cannot overcome; *no matter how bad it looks in the natural!* I don't care if you are facing the death sentence. I don't care if the mob is hunting you. I don't care if the KGB, FBI and the IRS are after you! This one revelation will bring you through to victory!

When we see the word "infirmities" in this scripture, most people only think of sickness or disease. Don't get me wrong — those *are* major infirmities — but there are other infirmities that are included also. Sometimes you're facing a crisis with your children or a crisis with your marriage. Other times you're facing a crisis with your neighbor or a crisis with your finances. These are all types of infirmities. That's why God inspired Paul to write verse 26, *"Likewise, the Holy Spirit helps us with our infirmities."* (Rom 8:26)

What does the Holy Spirit help us do with our infirmities? He comes to help you get rid of them, not build a Holiday Inn for them!

A Christian's Number One Infirmity

I had the privilege of knowing Dr. John G. Lake's daughter and son-in-law before they passed away. They were good friends of mine. And I heard them preach in Los Angeles at a meeting called: Secrets of Intercession. Wilford Reidt, Dr. Lake's son-in law was on the platform just talking a little bit and all of a sudden he began to speak with a fresh authority. He said, "The main infirmity of the Church is not sickness or the lack of money. The main infirmity of the Church is ignorance."

What a truthful statement! One of the greatest infirmities in the body of Christ is not that we don't have a will to do what is right, it's that we don't know what to do!

Even if you're a real good Bible student and you're faithful to your devotions, you'll still experience situations in life where you don't know what to do. You may know four or five scriptures that could apply to the situation, but which one will turn what your facing into a victorious situation and bless everybody involved? For instance, there's a scripture in Proverbs that says, *"He that findeth a wife findeth a good thing...,"* (Proverbs 18:22) but not knowing *who* and *when* is an infirmity!

It's an infirmity to not know which direction to turn or which scripture to apply to a specific situation. It is an infirmity to not know the specific will of God. The Holy Spirit helps you with that kind of infirmity. He illuminates the verse that applies to the situation you are facing and He makes it come alive to you.

Glowing Scriptures

Sometimes I hear people say, "That scripture jumped off the page at me!" I don't normally look for glowing scriptures for my guidance, but if one glows, I'll receive it!

When the Holy Spirit illuminates a scripture to you, it becomes a specific word from God. Praying in tongues helps these things come to you. It helps you to accurately express before God the inquiring and questioning that is in your spirit. And He likes to respond to you in specifics.

How To Overcome The Homebuyer's Blues

It's nice to know that it's God's will for you to own a home, but are you buying the right one? When you're investing $150,000, you have to know what you're getting into, my friend! It's not like buying a piece of bubble gum! When you sign your name on that loan, you're going to spend thirty, forty or maybe even fifty years paying that thing off. You don't want to be in a house that's not right for you! If you pray in tongues a lot, when you walk up the driveway, you'll be sensitive enough to hear God say, "No, don't buy it," or, "Yes, It's for you!"

Don't Go Overboard

Don't go overboard with what I'm saying. Sometimes people think they've got to ask God about everything. You don't need to say, "Is it okay to have some bubble gum, God?" Or, "what flavor should I buy today?" Buy whatever you want! Don't bother God with questions like, "Should I have Big Red or Juicy Fruit?" Buy whatever kind makes your taste buds jump and enjoy it!

"God, am I supposed to eat lunch today?"

Of course He want's you to eat lunch! That's why He made apples, vegetables and cows; so you can eat them! Don't bug God with questions like that! That's religious!

Just buy yourself a nice juicy steak or a ripe piece of fruit and make a lot of noise when you're eating it! God made food for you to enjoy! You don't need to ask God about things like that unless you know He wants you to go on a fast.

If God wants you to go on a fast, then keep your mouth shut! Don't run around saying, "I'm fasting. I can't eat today!" If you're going to groan and complain like that, just eat! Fasting should not be a disease that makes everybody around you depressed!

Making Major Decisions

"Likewise the Spirit helpeth our infirmities..." *(Romans 8:26)* Notice that the word "infirmities" here is plural. That means He helps us with *ALL* of our infirmities, not just one or two of them. He helps us in every area of life; physically, mentally and spiritually.

When you're making major decisions in life, always inquire of the Lord. Ask Him in your native language and then pray in tongues to take care of the specifics. If you don't get a good solid "Yes" just keep praying in tongues and praying with your understanding until you get a direct answer. You won't make bad decisions that way. God doesn't want you to make bad decisions, He wants you to make *wise* decisions.

Praying For Things You Were Not Expecting

"Likewise the Spirit also helpeth our infirmities, for we know not what we should pray as we ought...." (Romans 8:26)

God gave you tongues because you don't always know how to pray the right way. Sometimes, when you're praying in tongues, the Spirit will lead you into praying for something that your mind never thought of praying for; or sometimes He will have you pray for something that you thought you had already prayed through. All of a sudden, the Spirit of God will boil up from inside and move you to pray about something you were not expecting.

You see, The Holy Spirit knows the future. Sometimes He'll move you to pray in order to stop something tragic from happening to you. He also knows when there is going to be a lot of bombardment over what He wants you to do, so He will move you to pray to make sure you won't be touched, bothered or distracted when you walk through the fray. When the Holy Spirit prepares your insides ahead of time, instead of the hardship stopping or distracting you, you'll be prepared for it and you'll keep right on going.

Words In Your Native Language

Sometimes when you're praying in tongues, words in your native language will pop out. That's the Holy Spirit helping your mind to be edified while you're in prayer.

When you're praying on behalf of another, you sometimes won't know what you're praying about. You'll just have to trust God and make yourself available to be used as an intercessor. In those situations, you won't know what you prayed for until you get to Heaven.

The Holy Spirit works mainly by the power of words. Things move, appear and disappear when the words that you pray are inspired by the Holy Spirit. When God speaks through you and says, "No," things will disappear. When God speaks through you and says, "Yes," things will begin to show up.

Why Am I praying This?

Have you ever been praying for your husband, your wife or over your family and thought, "Why am I praying this?" That's the Holy Spirit helping you to pray! I've prayed things over my ministry and thought, "We're in peace right now, nothing bad is happening, why am I praying this?" But all of a sudden it just comes up in my spirit. I've learned by experience; if I don't yield to it, there will come a day when I wish I had!

If you wait until the battle begins in the natural, you'll have to fight with your soul's reactions as well as with the situation. I'll tell you from experience, that's hard work! It's good to get your prayer work done before you actually step into a major situation. That's why I always encourage people to pray a lot before they go on a missions trip. That way, when they get there, the spiritual work is almost complete except for the little bit that needs to be done while they're there. They just walk through the trip and have fun.

We do this before our campmeetings. We pray and we pray and we pray! By the time we get to the first service, we just jump into the meeting without a lot of work and we enjoy the blessings of God.

Praying The Perfect Will Of God

So when we don't know how to pray, we can always trust the Holy Spirit to pray through us in tongues and in our native language. He knows exactly what needs to be done and He will help us pray according to the perfect will of God.

There are times when people come up and ask me to pray with them about something. I don't know their situation but I want God to help them so I say, "Father, I lift them up to you, in Jesus' name..." and then I just let the Holy Spirit pray through me in tongues. When I pray in tongues, I know I'm praying correctly for the situation.

I know you are effected emotionally when you go through tragedy, but your emotions don't do a lot to move God. It is faith that moves Him. Praying in your natural language won't always be enough to solve the problem either. Your human vocabulary doesn't contain enough words to adequately pray for the situation. You need to get down on your knees and begin to let the Holy Spirit pray through you in tongues.

The Holy Spirit Is Praying Through You

Always remember, you are not praying to get through to God, you're allowing the Holy Spirit to pray through you for the purpose of effecting a change in the heavens and in the natural.

It says in the later half of verse 26, *"but the Spirit itself maketh intercession for us..."* This should really read, *"but the Spirit Himself..."* because the Holy Spirit is not an "it," He's a person.

The Holy Spirit will pray for you when nobody else will. You are never without prayer. Sometimes He'll pray all by Himself or sometimes through someone that is concerned about you, but most of the time He'll pray through you.

The Devil Is The Source Of Your Trouble

Some people think that the Holy Spirit's only job is to give you comfort while you're in the midst of your infirmities. He does that, but the main comfort He brings is a deliverance out of your trouble. The Holy Spirit wants to help you get out of your trouble. He wants to give you knowledge that will solve your problem. He comes to show you a way of escape. He shows you what to do and say in precarious situations. He makes power available to kill the disease that is tormenting your body.

"But Brother Roberts, I think God gave me this trouble to teach me something."

Get it straight in your head right now! The devil is the source of everything evil in your life! All trouble, someway, somehow, originates from his puny little heart and mind! The devil will do anything he can to keep you in bondage. He will even quote you the words of an old religious song! Religious spirits will try to murder you while you're singing "Amazing Grace!"

The Bible declares boldly that, *"Every Good gift and every Perfect gift, is from above, and comes down from the Father of lights, with whom there is no variation or shadow of turning."* James 1:17 (NKJ)

God says, "I've come to help you get free, I've come to deliver you, I've come to give you help in a time of need."

Stubborn Strongholds

There have been times in my life when I've felt like saying, "Lord, I've prayed the prayer of faith, I've bound, I've loosed, I've submitted, I've sung, I've done cartwheels across the lawn in front of my house — I've prayed every kind of prayer that's available and yet this stronghold is still laughing at me and punching me in the nose! Hello!

Has all of heaven gone to bed?" Have you ever felt like that? Thank God there's a prayer that solves all these kind of problems! When I feel that way, I'm so glad that I have been empowered by the Holy Spirit! I'm so glad He lives big inside of me! My help is not in my biceps, it's in the Spirit! All I have to do is just open my mouth and allow the Holy Spirit to pray through me in tongues and eventually those stubborn strongholds will come down!

Pray In Tongues When You're Tired

Sometimes there come storms that hit you when you're not expecting them and your mind doesn't just react – it faints. You get real grumpy and you don't want to think much. You don't believe anything and you don't even want to read the Bible. I've been there; I know what it's like.

I don't care how strong you are or how long you've been walking with God, there will be times when the storms of life will be so overwhelming that your mind will faint. There will be times in the natural when you can't get yourself together enough to pray by your understanding. But the Spirit of God will bubble up inside of you when your soul has fainted and He will Help you pray. Thank God for the unknown tongue. When your mind faints, tongues will flow right out of your belly and begin working to strengthen you and change the situation.

The Devil's Multiple Warheads

At times in my life there has come what I call multiple warheads. The devil can't get me with just one bomb anymore so he comes at me in multiples. Have you ever experienced those kinds of attacks?

After a few heated battles, you'll become a veteran in war and the devil's attacks won't bother you as much. I'm immune to most of the devil's attacks. It doesn't bother me when people want to fight with me. I've been through money wars, rumor wars and spirit wars — I've been through every kind of war you can think of. These kinds of wars don't bother me anymore. When they come at me I just say, "Get a number and get in line! Next!"

The first couple of times I went through a war it was a big deal, but after the third or fourth time, it didn't register anymore. I just went out and enjoyed a delightful meal.

Some of you are not at that place yet and you're facing some major battles. What happens when you're in trouble and no one is around at midnight to help you? What happens when the one you're calling doesn't give you that word of encouragement that gets you through another hour? What happens when those who call you on the phone only give you more bad reports? What happens when your soul constantly reminds you of the pain that you're in and not of the peace you should have? What happens when your nice smiling neighbor turns into a demon possessed neighbor at night? What happens when your friends try to help you out but they unknowingly cooperate with the negative atmosphere or pressure that is against you?

I've been to the place where people were trying to do the best they knew to encourage me but they just couldn't do it. That's why we have the wonderful world of tongues, my friend.

When your soul faints, when your support team is not there in a crisis of need, the Holy Spirit boils up inside of you. All you have to do is yield to the Holy Spirit and let Him take charge. Let Him rise up big inside of you and He will pull you through.

It would be nice if God came down and sovereignly fixed our problems — sometimes He does. But most of the time He works through the wonderful world of tongues.

9

THE GIFT OF TONGUES & THE GIFT OF INTERPRETATION OF TONGUES

But the manifestation of the Spirit is given to every man to profit withal. For to one is given by the Spirit the word of wisdom; to another the word of knowledge by the same Spirit; To another faith by the same Spirit; to another the gifts of healing by the same Spirit; To another the working of miracles; to another prophecy; to another discerning of spirits; TO ANOTHER DIVERS KINDS OF TONGUES; TO ANOTHER THE INTERPRETATION OF TONGUES: But all these worketh that one and the selfsame Spirit, dividing to every man severally as he will.

1 Cor 12:7-11 (KJV)

In this verse, the apostle Paul lists nine separate gifts of the Spirit. Two of these nine gifts, the gift of diverse kinds of tongues and the gift of interpretation of tongues, are married and function as one. You can't have one without the other. When there comes a tongue into the congregation, there should always come an interpretation.

When these two gifts manifest together, they have the same effect as the gift of prophecy. The gift of tongues, the gift of the interpretation of tongues and the gift of prophecy are all gifts that God uses to communicate to people. They are known as the "utterance gifts."

Tongues For Public Assembly

When the gift of tongues and the gift of interpretation of tongues manifest in a church service, it will often come into the room without warning. It may come upon somebody in the congregation, someone on the pastoral team or it may even come upon the pastor. Suddenly the gift of tongues will manifest in a language that is unknown to those in the room. If you are discerning in the spirit, you'll sense when these gifts are present in a meeting.

Just because you're sensing a "tongue" doesn't mean you're supposed to give it, however. If you don't have an unction, just remain still. When the unction comes on you, you'll have a strong knowing. It will feel like it's boiling up from within you like water boiling on the stove; everything will be real calm in the pot but as the heat gets hotter, it will bubble up and overflow. An unction will just keep coming up in you stronger and stronger until you just can't hold it back anymore. Boom! It will suddenly come out, and sometimes you will be the most surprised person in the room! You'll think, "My God, what did I do? Did I do something wrong?" No, you were just used by God to manifest the gift of tongues. Now those in the congregation are supposed to wait for someone to give the interpretation.

You may wait for a few minutes and then, all of a sudden, the same person who gave the tongue may give the interpretation, or it may be somebody clear on the other side of the room.

When a public tongue comes like that, there is to be an interpretation every time so that everyone in the room can understand. (1 Cor 14:27-28) When you have a nice, marijuana smoking sinner in the church, he should not be left saying to himself, "What in the world was that?"

Won't They Think You're Crazy?

"But Pastor Roberts, if an unbeliever comes into the church and they hear someone speaking in tongues, won't they think you're crazy?"

No. Tongues is a sign to those who aren't saved, as well as to those who haven't received the fullness of Holy Spirit yet. First Corinthians 14:22 says:

"Wherefore tongues are a sign, not to them that believe, but to them that believe not."

1 Cor 14:22 (KJV)

Some churches are embarrassed about the gift of tongues and the gift of the interpretation of tongues so they push them over into a corner. Don't ever be afraid that tongues and interpretation will spook your visitors. Tongues is a sign to them. Usually, the people that get upset about tongues in the assembly are *Christians*, not sinners! It's true that there are times when tongues should not be the forefront activity in a service, but you should never be embarrassed about it either. In 1 Cor 14:39 Paul said, *"Therefore, brethren, desire earnestly to prophesy, and do not forbid to speak with tongues."* Paul also said, *"I thank God I pray in tongues more than you all..."* (1 Cor 14:18) That means Paul prayed in tongues a whole lot and he was not ashamed of it.

Tongues are a sign to nonbelievers. Tongues will encourage them, inspire them and help them increase their awareness of God.

What If There's No Interpretation?

Tongues and the interpretation of tongues equal the gift of prophecy. When someone flows in the gift of prophecy, there will be no tongues. Prophecy is a divine utterance in the native language of the people, so the congregation can be edified and the church built up.

In the same way, God uses the gifts of tongues and the interpretation of tongues to communicate to His people, to encourage them, to cover them, to correct them and to admonish them. So whenever there comes a public tongue, there should always come an interpretation.

"But Pastor Roberts, what if somebody doesn't give the interpretation? What do we do?"

You just go on with the service, but ten times out of ten, if it's a true tongue, there's an interpretation in the room somewhere. If the interpretation doesn't come, it might be because the person that received it is scared to give it and they are holding it back. When they say "no" and they keep pushing it down, they grieve the Spirit of God. When that happens, the Spirit of God will fall on somebody else to give it. That's why it sometimes takes a little bit longer than usual to get the interpretation.

Usually, when a tongue and an interpretation comes, if the congregation is fluent in spiritual things and there is no fear among them, the interpretation will come almost before the tongue is finished. The person interpreting will just start bubbling over with the interpretation. That's the way it often works when there is a fluency in the congregation and there's no embarrassment about the gifts of the Spirit.

Leadership Can Usually Interpret

When there is no interpretation in the congregation, if the leadership will reach out to God, they can usually get it. As the pastor of the church, I can usually get the interpretation of a tongue, whether I'm unctioned to give it or not. I usually get the gist of it and many times I get it word for word. But if I were to interpret all the time, my congregation would never do it. They'd just wait for me to give the interpretation. That's why I don't do it all the time.

Sometimes there will come a series of tongues and interpretations, one after the other.

"Well why can't God say everything all at once?" Because He doesn't want to.

It's like when I'm overseas preaching in Russia or in China. When I get up and I say, "How is everybody doing?" the interpreter translates my short sentence and then waits for me to give the next one. The interpreter has to break my sermon down into little sections in order to speak it out accurately to the people. God does the same thing when He's communicating to His people through the gifts of tongues and interpretation.

Don't Be Afraid To Flow

When you're being used in the gift of tongues and interpretation, don't let your mind talk you out of what you're hearing in your spirit. Sometimes your mind will say, "Everyone thinks you're crazy! They're not receiving what you're saying! You're nuts, you're missing it, you're just goofy!" When that happens, you have to tell your mind to be still. You have to quiet your mind down so your spirit can have freedom to do what it needs to do.

In my church, I see the Spirit of God fall on certain ones at certain times but they're too afraid of making a mistake to speak it out. I can almost hear them thinking, "Well what if I'm not right?"

If your tongue or interpretation is not quite right, I won't embarrass you! I'll just help you out a little bit if it is necessary or, I'll let the Spirit of God make the adjustments. God can take care of things without my help at all and He does a much better job than I ever could.

If God boils up in you during a meeting and gives you a tongue and an interpretation, just go ahead and give it.

"Is there any special time to give it?"

Yes, when He comes on you to give it.

"What if you're in the middle of your sermon?"

If it's truly the Holy Spirit and He boils up in someone, it doesn't bother me at all. I'll just be quiet for a moment and let the Holy Spirit talk to the people directly instead of through me. But normally, if you have a flow of the Holy Spirit in your church, you can feel the timing of it. You can usually sense when the Spirit of God is going to move in a service.

Many churches today don't experience the blessing of the utterance gifts because they don't make time for them to manifest during the service.

10

INTERPRETING YOUR PERSONAL PRAYER LANGUAGE

In 1 Corinthians 14:13, Paul writes: *"Wherefore let him that speaketh in an unknown tongue pray that he may interpret."* Interpret what? What he prays in the unknown tongue.

This verse does not pertain to the gift of tongues and the gift of the interpretation of tongues for public assembly. The apostle Paul is writing here about interpreting your own personal prayer language.

How do you receive an interpretation of your personal prayer language? The same way that you receive an interpretation of tongues in a public setting; through the operation of the gift of interpretation of tongues.

The first thing you have to do when you're praying in tongues is make time for the interpretation to come back to you. Some people have never had their prayer language interpreted back to them by the Holy Spirit because they have never made time for the interpretation to come.

The Lord may speak to you in great detail about what you've been praying about, or He may just let you know the gist of it. At times an interpretation will be available, but if you don't give time for it, it won't come.

Sometimes while I'm praying in tongues, I instantly understand what I'm saying. You may have had that happen to you, but you didn't know what it was. It may have seemed like your mind was giving you some nice little verses and you didn't register it as the Holy Spirit interpreting your prayer language.

Oral Roberts Explains How He Built ORU

Oral Roberts, the high-profile healing evangelist who blazed a trail of miracles across postwar America, tells how interpreting his personal prayer language helped him build a university for the Lord in Tulsa, Oklahoma.

As Oral was walking across a cow pasture one day and praying in tongues, the Lord said to him, "Oral, I want you buy the land you're walking on, and build Me a university." He knew it was God speaking to him, but he had no idea how to build something as large as a university. So he walked back and forth across the field praying in tongues and then waited for the interpretation. When the interpretation came, Oral spoke out in English what he had been praying in tongues. That's how he knew what to do and when to do it. That's how he found out how to raise enough money to get it done. Oral allowed the Spirit of God to interpret back to his mind what he was communicating and talking to God about in tongues.

Today, Oral Roberts University (ORU) has 22 major buildings and is valued at more than $250 million dollars and over 10,000 students have passed through its classrooms.

Interpreting Your Tongues Helps Your Mind

Let's look at 1 Corinthians 14:14 more closely:

For if I pray in a tongue, my spirit prays, but my understanding is unfruitful. What is the conclusion then? I will pray with the spirit, and I will also pray with the understanding. I will sing with the spirit, and I will also sing with the understanding.

1 Cor 14:14-15 (NKJ)

Notice that Paul says, *"For if I pray in a tongue, my spirit prays, but my understanding is unfruitful...."* In other words, Paul is saying that when you pray in tongues, your mind does not understand what you're saying. That's why it is important to pray every day in your native language as well as in tongues. You should sing everyday in your native language and in tongues too. It helps your mind stay in touch with what is happening in your spirit.

Interpreting your own prayer language also helps your mind. Interpreting what the Holy Spirit has been praying through you can help you determine the true spiritual condition of your life. Your mind doesn't know what your spirit knows and one way for your mind to find out is by listening to the interpretation of your private tongues.

Your private interpretation does not usually come like a public interpretation. Tongues and interpretation in a public assembly comes real bold and real obvious. In your private prayer life, an interpretation may come up real quietly inside of you. It will boil up out of your spirit, and then enter into your mind. When you speak it out, there may or may not be an authoritative tone to it.

Interpreting your prayer language will help keep your mind normal. When people don't renew their mind, they get a little off center. They sometimes get spooky and begin to lose touch with reality. If they would renew their mind with the Word of God, pray and sing a lot in their native language and allow the Holy Spirit to interpret their prayer language back to them, their mind would not be as unfruitful.

11

DIVERSITIES OF TONGUES

And God hath set some in the church, first apostles, secondarily prophets, thirdly teachers, after that miracles, then gifts of healings, helps, governments, DIVERSITIES OF TONGUES.

1 Cor 12:28 (KJV)

This verse contains a lineup of things that Jesus "set" into the church. These things are not just for private use in your prayer closet. Jesus ordained these things to be *publicly* manifest in the church! He set, apostles, prophets, teachers and after that miracles!

Miracles belong in the church, my brother and sister. They are not just for the mission field or the evangelistic crusade. *God* has *"set"* these things into the church and man has no right to excommunicate them!

When God "sets" something into the church, it means He wants them to have a *residential existence*. In other words, these things are not just supposed to have "visitation rights," they are supposed to dwell residentially in our midst.

"But brother Roberts, these things are not in the church that I go to!"

Then you're not in a church, my friend, *you're in a club!*

Notice the rest of this verse: *"And God hath set...in the church...gifts of healings, helps, governments and DIVERSITIES OF TONGUES."*

The word *"diversities"* here means: different kinds of tongues. There are different types of tongues that do different things.

One guy said to me, "We have diversity of tongues in our church. We've got some Russians that speak in Russian. We've got some French and they speak some French and we've got some Hispanics and they speak in Spanish."

That's not what this verse is talking about at all! The term "diversities of tongues" here is referring to the various kinds of utterances that bubble up from within your spirit by the supernatural power of God.

Rivers Of Living Water

Jesus made reference to the diversities of tongues when He spoke about the various rivers of the Holy Spirit that would flow from the heart of the believer. In the gospel of John we read:

...Jesus stood and cried out, saying, "If anyone thirsts, let him come to Me and drink. "He who believes in Me, as the Scripture has said, out of his heart will flow RIVERS of living water." But this He spoke concerning the Spirit, whom those believing in Him would receive; for the Holy Spirit was not yet given, because Jesus was not yet glorified.

John 7:37-39 (NKJ)

Notice that Jesus said, "*...out of his heart will flow RIVERS of living water.*" The word "rivers" is plural meaning *more than one river.* And where do these rivers come from? From the Holy Spirit within you! They bubble up from your belly in various forms of tongues. The Holy Spirit will bring different moves or different flows up out of your spirit.

Various Kinds Of Tongues

Most Bible teachers today only teach about one type of tongue; tongues for personal edification. That's why most Christians are stuck in one zone when it comes to praying in tongues. They don't teach on the diversities of tongues that God makes available to His people.

Tongues for personal edification is important, but what about tongues of intercession? Diversities of tongues need to be taught in the Church so that the people can understand what they are and how to flow in them.

If you know about the different diversities of tongues that are available, you can step into them when the Spirit of God leads and get things done faster.

Many Christians today don't know that diversities of tongues are available to them. Some may know it by chapter and verse, but they don't know it experientially. When they begin to venture into the deeper things of God through praying in tongues, they withdraw themselves from different diversities because of fear or because of ignorance. That's why so many have troubles in their life that never seem to conclude. They don't know how to go deep enough in the Holy Spirit to find the answers to their problem.

The Holy Spirit knows what kind of utterance and expression is needed to bring you into victory. And He'll boil up inside of you various tongues for the various circumstances of life. The Holy Spirit also knows what kind of intensity and what level of divine authority is required in your prayer language in order to bring a change in the situation.

Sometimes, you'll be praying in your normal tongue and then it will suddenly change. When you experience that, your prayer language has just kicked into a new level of expression or you're beginning to intercede effectively on behalf of a situation that needs changing.

Don't Tamper With How It Comes Out!

When the Holy Spirit boils up a tongue inside of your spirit, don't tamper with it! If you get more intense than you should, if you act more calm than you should, if you weep when He is not weeping — if you rework your tongues in any way — it will effect your victory. You must allow your tongues to come out of you the way He gives them to you.

You may also lose your victory if you infect your praying with your emotions, your paranoia or your political reworkings. I've learned this by experience. When I wouldn't pray the way that God boiled up in my spirit, I'd lose my victory for a season. When I prayed in a way that made all my preacher friends happy, I would leave with their blessing, but I didn't leave with victory in my life. Thank God I got delivered from that stupidity! I had to get to the place where I wanted victory in my private life more than I wanted men's approval.

You will have to come to that place too! In order to flow in the diversities of tongues, you have to be willing to allow the Holy Spirit to flow however He wants. If He wants you to pray real bold and strong to change a situation, you'll have to obey. You can't back off because of atmospheric oppression or because of fear that someone will think you're weird. You have to come to the place where you want victory more than you want your dinner date! You have to come to the place where you want your crazy children living right more than you want everybody to think that you're okay!

Tongues Opens The World Of The Spirit

You also have to develop the ability to cooperate with the Holy Spirit when He bubbles up new words in your prayer language. Just like English opens up the world that speaks English and German opens up the world that speaks German, praying in tongues opens up the world of the spirit to you.

When I go to Russia, I usually take an interpreter along to help me. When I arrive at the airport in Moscow, I become dependent upon my interpreter as soon as I get off the plane because I don't know Russian.

My interpreter has the ability to get the job done, because he knows the language. Sometimes my interpreter will be real nice to people and talk to them real sweet in Russian and other times you'd think he's a part of the Red Army about to attack! When I ask my interpreter what's going on he just says, "I'm taking care of it."

Sometimes he'll inquire about something and other times he will be giving commands. I can usually tell what he's doing by the sound of his words, but I don't know what he's actually saying.

The same way my interpreter speaks for me, when I'm in Russia, the Holy Spirit speaks through me when I'm in the spirit.

When I am preaching with an interpreter, for the most part I ignore the interpreter and keep my eyes upon whom I'm speaking to. I have to just trust that my interpreter is going to accurately translate what I have said to the people. The whole world can be opened up to me through helpers called: interpreters.

The Holy Spirit Is Our Interpreter

The Holy Spirit works the same way with you in the world of the Spirit. When you lean upon the Holy Spirit in your praying, diversities of tongues will come through you and your tone will change as well as your utterances.

The Holy Spirit has expressions too, folks. That's why monotone praying in tongues usually puts you in a dead end street. It may work for you a little, but it won't do much for you because you've contained it. You need to begin to allow the Spirit of God to manifest diversities of tongues through you privately and at times publicly.

Tongues To God & Tongues With God

I have heard some people say, "Well, tongues is to speak to God with." (1 Cor 14:2) That's true, but the Bible says that there are *diversities* of tongues, which means different kinds of tongues for different things. (1 Cor 12:28) If all you do is limit your tongues to just speaking to God or building yourself up, you'll never get into the depths of what God has for you.

You have to understand that when you're speaking in tongues, sometimes you're speaking to God and sometimes you're working with God. When you're working with God in the spirit, the Holy Spirit will use your prayer language to effect things in the earth. That's where intercessory prayer comes from.

Most Bible teachers today only teach about the kind of tongues that people speak to God with. They don't know much about praying *with* God.

Now when you're praying *with* God, you're not lifting your voice and asking Him for things, you're yielding your mouth to the Holy Spirit so He can make intercession through you. The Holy Spirit can pray through you either in tongues or in your native language.

Some Examples Of Praying With God

When you yield to the Holy Spirit, sometimes there will come what I call "breakthrough tongues." I used to use the term "warfare tongues," but certain people got mad at me because they couldn't find that word in the Bible. So now I just call them breakthrough tongues. I really don't care what you call them, just use them.

In James chapter 5 verse 16 we read: *"The effective, FERVENT prayer of a righteous man avails much."* (NKJ) Sometimes the Holy Spirit will boil up in fervent tongues in order to bring a breakthrough in a certain situation. Strong tongues are the spiritual battering ram that the Holy Spirit uses to overthrow the strongholds of the enemy.

When you start praying in real strong tongues, some of the old-time Pentecostals will get upset and say, "How dare you yell at God in tongues?" I usually respond by saying, "Have you ever been in your prayer closet just worshiping the Lord when all of a sudden the Holy Spirit boils up tongues in you that sound like a big old bear?"

"Well, yes," they usually answer.

"Were you talking to God when you were praying like that?"

"Well, no."

"Was it the Holy Spirit praying through you?"

"Yes."

"Then don't get mad when I pray in strong tongues."

Breakthrough Tongues

I want you to understand the different diversities of tongues so you can yield to them when the Holy Spirit brings them up inside you.

That's why sometimes I will say to people by the Spirit, "Change that tongue. You're praying in the wrong tongue to get victory in that situation."

You can't be praying in tongues of edification when you need a breakthrough. You've got to have something more.

You have to be careful that you don't pray in those same old boring tongues all the time. If you constantly pray in the same monotone tongue and your utterances never fluctuate, you've got a problem. Your fluency has been broken and you're stuck in a rut.

Groanings, Travailings & Weepings

Many times when you are praying, one type of tongue will give way to another operation of the Holy Spirit's communication and working. Sometimes groanings, travailings and weepings will begin to come up out of your spirit. (Rom 8:26, Gal 4:19; Ps 126:5-6) Why are they called groanings, travailings and weepings? Because that's what they sound like. These are some of the languages of heaven.

I have not heard much on these kinds of manifestations of the Holy Spirit, but they are real. They will come on you at times and you should know what they are and be willing to yield to them. Some of you have probably already yielded to these things but didn't know what to call them.

For a long time, speaking in tongues real bold made people feel nervous. But now that tongues is becoming a little more acceptable, we have to get comfortable with the groanings, travailings, weepings of the Spirit. These things will come periodically as the Spirit of God will lead and we have to know how to yield to them. Right now, the Holy Spirit wants to do these things a whole lot. There's a lot to groan, travail and cry about. There are many things that we are supposed to bring into the earth by the help of the Holy Spirit.

12

COMMON SENSE WITH THE USE OF TONGUES

In this chapter, I wanted to give you a few thoughts on the practical side of praying in tongues so it will be a blessing to you and not a hinderance.

First of all, when you're flowing in the gift of tongues and the gift of the interpretation of tongues, you've got to be sensitive to those you are speaking to. There have been times in my life when I've felt a "tongue" arise in my spirit, but I've had to prepare the people to receive it by explaining what was about to occur.

In the early years of my ministry, I received an invitation to speak at a first Baptist church in Hartford, Connecticut. I asked my secretary to call them and make sure they knew I was a full gospel preacher and that I spoke in tongues. To my surprise, they wanted me to come anyway and so I went.

In the middle of one of the night meetings, I felt a "tongue" arise in my spirit. I wanted the people to receive it so I did my best to prepare them for it.

"Folks, I'm from a full gospel background," I said, "we believe in the gifts of the Holy Spirit and one of them is about to manifest right now. Don't be afraid, just sit back, relax and receive."

After I gave the "tongue" and the interpretation, the people began shouting excitedly all over the room. They had never experienced anything like that before. When I gave the altar call, over 150 people came forward and received the baptism in the Holy Spirit with the evidence of speaking in tongues!

If I hadn't been sensitive to God and to the people, I wouldn't have experienced those wonderful results.

Do I Have To Pray Loud?

People often approach me after my meetings and ask, "Do I have to pray in tongues loud to be effective?"

"No," I tell them, "you just have to pray *fervently* to be effective." (Jas 5:16)

Praying *strong* doesn't always mean praying *loud*, my brother and sister. Praying strong means praying fervently with a voice of authority. That voice of authority comes from the confidence and freedom of a Spirit-filled life. I'm not against praying out loud in tongues where others can hear you, but I don't want to propagate a yelling contest, either.

In my meetings, we pray out loud in tongues and have a great time, but you can't pray like that in every environment. For example: when you are in a hospital room praying for someone, you can't pray and act like you're in a believer's meeting or they may take you to the 13th floor, strap a straightjacket on you and commit you into the psyche-ward! They'll say, "We have someone who became mentally ill while visiting another patient!" You have to know how to function according to the environment you're in. That's not compromising, that's just walking wisely before others and being a witness.

I was taught as a child to pray audibly enough for my ears to hear my voice. To me, that is still a good balance in most situations.

You Have To Be Relatable

Some Christians think they have to shout, jerk and have a volcanic explosion every time they speak in tongues! Always remember, the more spiritual you are, the more relatable you should be. God is in the business of drawing people to Himself, not blowing them away!

Praying in tongues and being spiritual should not keep you from doing what is right in the natural, either. In fact, it should help you do it better! If I had an employee that prayed so much in tongues that they didn't do a proper job, I'd fire them! Something is wrong with you if you cannot function in the natural world!

If you become superspiritual and spooky, you'll have no friends and you'll feel like everyone is against you. I've had to tell people to stop praying in tongues and go chop wood, get a job, or just talk in their native language for awhile. Sometimes people need a reality check — they have to learn how to be relatable so they can be fruitful in God's kingdom.

Some women who are married to unsaved husbands don't have it very easy. But if your unsaved husband comes home and all you do is pray in tongues and you never take care of the housework or your other responsibilities, why would he want to get saved and act like you?

Praying in tongues and being spiritual shouldn't keep you from being a good husband, a good wife, a good mother, a good child, a good employee or a good citizen!

No one who is truly spiritual is going to blow up a building in Oklahoma City! Nobody that prays in tongues and truly worships Jesus is going to gather a bunch of weapons and hide out in Waco, Texas! When someone goes "AWOL" in the name of religion, it effects all of us. People that do things like that are not even religious, *they're demon possessed*. They should be put in jail and rightfully punished!

13

HOW TO MINISTER THE BAPTISM IN THE HOLY SPIRIT

There are at least seven steps to successfully minister the baptism in the Holy Spirit with the evidence of speaking in other tongues. The seven steps are:

STEP ONE:

Help the person see that the Holy Spirit has already been poured out. (Acts 2:4)

The Holy Spirit was poured out on the day of Pentecost and this powerful gift has been available to believers ever since. Explain to the person that they don't have to beg for the gift of the Holy Spirit, all they have to do is receive it by faith.

STEP TWO :

Show the person receiving that if they are born-again, they are already qualified to receive the gift of the Holy Spirit.

Explain to them that they don't have to somehow clean up their life in order to receive the promise of the Spirit. It's a free gift. All they have to do is ask to receive it. (Lk 11:13)

STEP THREE:

Tell the person to expect to receive when you lay your hands on them.

The gift of the Holy Spirit is often imparted to believers through the laying on of hands. Before laying hands on them and praying, explain that it is not you who will baptize them with the Holy Spirit, but rather the Lord Jesus Christ. The laying on of hands only serves as a point of contact for them to release their faith.

STEP FOUR:

Explain to the person what is about to happen to them and that they are the one who is going to have to open their mouth to do the speaking.

The Holy Spirit will not do the speaking for them! The person receiving will have to open their mouth and yield to the inner flow of the Holy Spirit.

STEP FIVE:

Assure them that they will not receive a counterfeit spirit.

In Luke 11:11-13, Jesus said:

"If a son asks for bread from any father among you, will he give him a stone? Or if he asks for a fish, will he

give him a serpent instead of a fish? Or if he asks for an egg, will he offer him a scorpion? "If you then, being evil, know how to give good gifts to your children, how much more will your heavenly Father give the Holy Spirit to those who ask Him!"

Lk 11:11-13 (NKJ)

STEP SIX:

Encourage the person to speak out and act in faith.

Don't allow the person to speak anything in their native language. Tell them to open their mouth by faith and begin to pronounce the various syllables and sounds of their new personal prayer language.

STEP SEVEN:

Don't allow a crowd to gather around the person you are ministering to.

Onlookers create confusion and often hinder the person you are praying for from receiving the gift of the Holy Spirit.

14

HOW TO RECEIVE THE HOLY SPIRIT AND SPEAK WITH TONGUES

And they were all filled with the Holy Spirit and began to speak with other tongues, AS THE SPIRIT GAVE THEM UTTERANCE.

Acts 2:4 (NKJ)

When seeking the baptism in the Holy Spirit, it's important to recognize that the disciples spoke in tongues *"as the Spirit gave them utterance."* (Acts 2:4) What does that mean? It means that in their spirit they began to hear the voice of the Holy Spirit giving them utterances. They heard the utterances on the inside, but they had to open their mouth and speak them out.

In order to speak in your new prayer language, you have to get your mind quiet so you can hear what the Holy

Spirit is saying to you inwardly. Some people only hear one sound and say it over and over. That's a good start.

When you receive the baptism in the Holy Spirit, there is no need for dramatic emotion, jerking or falling down. It's just like saying, "One, two, three," and you're off, speaking in tongues. What happens? You hear new words on the inside, where the Holy Spirit speaks to your spirit, and you begin to speak them out in faith. It's that simple.

Now that you know all the reasons why the devil doesn't want you to speak in tongues, it's time to receive the baptism in the Holy Spirit. Just pray the prayer on following page out loud and then step out in faith and begin to speak in your new heavenly language.

Dear Lord Jesus,

I believe that You are the One who baptizes with the Holy Spirit. I ask you to baptize me with the Holy Spirit now. I receive the fullness of Your precious Spirit by faith and I will now begin to speak with other tongues. In Jesus' mighty name I pray, Amen.

Signed_____

Now that you are speaking in tongues, I want to know it. Please write me and describe your experience with tongues. Please include your name, address, phone number and e-mail address.

You overcome the devil by "...the blood of the Lamb and the word of your testimony...." (Rev 12:11)

Send me your testimony about tongues today!

I also want you to include any prayer requests you might have. Send them to me so I can join with you in the powerful prayer of agreement. **It's time to get militant about your life!**

WANT MORE?

How I Learned To Pray: Basic Laws Of Prayer

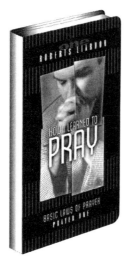

Learn how to develop a powerful prayer life! In Volume One, Pastor Roberts shares the lessons he was taught as a boy that he still lives by today. It is this instruction that has produced the fruit you see in his ministry, and it will produce fruit in your life too!

6 Audio Tapes: A0041
$30.00

Lost In The Spirit: And Don't Want To Come Back!

Are you ready to take your prayer life to the next level? Volume two of this series reveals a place of prayer where time and circumstances are no longer distractions. This place of initmacy and power in the spirit is just waiting to be discovered!

6 Audio Tapes: A0042
$30.00

Special Price – 2 for $50 / *Offer No. F0021*

To place an order call (949) 833-3555
or visit our website at: www.robertsliardon.org

FREE BOOK!

Knowing People By The Spirit
by Pastor Roberts Liardon

Knowing People By The Spirit will teach you how to be led by the Spirit and not by your suspicions. It will show you how to keep the words, or the opinions, of men from becoming stronger than what you sense by the Spirit.

If you want to fully cooperate with God in these last days, you'll have to go beyond what you know about people in the natural and you'll have to know them by the Spirit.

To recieve a **FREE** copy of *Knowing People By The Spirit,* write today! Roberts Liardon Ministries, P.O. Box 30710, Laguna Hills, CA 92654. For faster service use our world-wide website at: www.robertsliardon.org, include your full name, address, city, state, zip code, area code and phone number.

Seven reasons you should attend Spirit Life Bible College

1. SLBC is a **spiritual school** with an academic support; not an academic school with a spiritual touch.

2. SLBC teachers are **successful ministers** in their own right. Pastor Roberts Liardon will not allow failure to be imparted into his students.

3. SLBC is a member of **Oral Roberts University Educational Fellowship** and is **fully accredited** by the International Christian Accreditation Association.

4. SLBC hosts monthly seminars with some of the **world's greatest** ministers who add another element, anointing and impartation to the students' lives.

5. Roberts Liardon understands your commitment to come to SLBC and commits himself to students by **ministering weekly** in classroom settings.

6. SLBC provides **hands-on** ministerial training.

7. SLBC provides ministry opportunity through its **post-graduate placement program**.

Send for your **FREE Video** of Spirit Life Bible College today!

Spirit Life Partner

Wouldn't It Be Great...

- If you could send 500 missionaries to the nations of the earth?
- If you could travel 250,000 air miles, boldly preaching the Word of God in 93 nations?
- If you could strengthen and train the next generation of God's leaders?
- If you could translate 23 books and distribute them into 37 countries?

Roberts Liardon

Roberts Liardon Ministries is sending Gospel missionaries to the hard and remote places of the earth!

...Now You Can!

Maybe you can't go, but by supporting this ministry every month, your gift can help to communicate the gospel around the world.

-------------------- CLIP ALONG LINE & MAIL TO ROBERTS LIARDON MINISTRIES. --------------------

☐ **YES!!** Pastor Roberts, I want to support your work in the kingdom of God by becoming a **SPIRIT LIFE PARTNER.** Please find enclosed my first monthly gift.

Name _____

Address _____

City _____ State _____ Zip _____

Phone (_____) _____

SPIRIT LIFE PARTNER AMOUNT: $ _____

☐ Check / Money Order ☐ VISA ☐ American Express ☐ Discover ☐ MasterCard

☐☐☐☐ ☐☐☐☐ ☐☐☐☐ ☐☐☐☐

Name On Card _____ Exp. Date ____/____/____

Signature _____ Date ____/____/____

Roberts Liardon Ministries

P.O. Box 30710 ♦ Laguna Hills, CA 92654 ♦ (949) 833-3555 ♦ Fax (949) 833.9555 ♦ www.robertsliardon.org

Not Just Another Ministry Magazine!

- It's got power! That's right, words are power.
- It's design allows you to place the magazine in your Bible and carry it with you to church or work.
- It provides front line reports from believers just like you who are kicking the devil's behind every day.

- It provides opportunities for your personal involvement. It's not enough for you receive all the revelatory truths it contains and keep all this power to yourself. Use it to encourage, exhort and build-up your friends.

Call or Write Today for your
FREE SUBSCRIPTION
(949) 833-3555

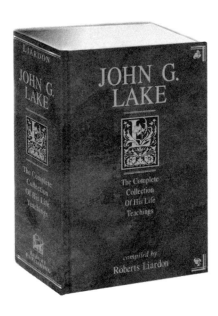

If you desire for Pastor Roberts Liardon to speak in your church, contact one of the following locations.

EUROPE
Roberts Liardon Ministries
P.O. Box 295
Welwyn Garden City
AL7 2ZG
England
011-44-1707-327-222

SOUTH AFRICA
Roberts Liardon Ministries
P.O. Box 3155
Kimberely 8300
South Africa
011-27-53-832-1207

AUSTRALIA
Roberts Liardon Ministries
P.O. Box 7
Kingsgrove, NSW
1480
Australia
011-61-500-555-056

USA
P.O. Box 30710
Laguna Hills, California, USA
92654-0710
Telephone: (949) 833-3555
Fax: (949) 833-9555
Visit our website at: www.robertsliardon.org